NIGHT WALK

Storey Publishing

Are You Ready to EXPLORE THE NIGHT?

When you step outside after dark, you'll find a whole nighttime world waiting. Lean your head back and look up at the moon or count stars. Listen for owls in the trees. Search for swooping bats and fluttering moths overhead. Grab a flashlight, open your front door, and discover what can happen on a night walk!

THINGS TO BRING IN YOUR BACKPACK

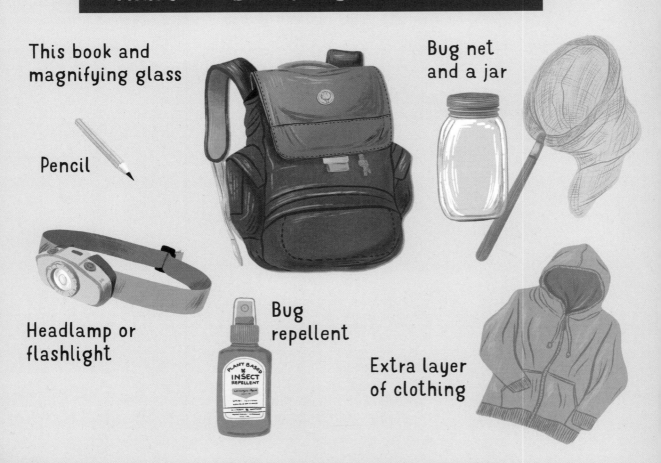

This book and magnifying glass

Pencil

Headlamp or flashlight

Bug net and a jar

Bug repellent

PLANT BASED INSECT REPELLENT

Extra layer of clothing

HOW TO HAVE FUN WITH THIS BOOK

Catch a FIREFLY

Count SHOOTING STARS

Go on a SCAVENGER HUNT

Make a snack for MOTHS

Use the MAGNIFYING GLASS for a closer look

HOOT like an owl

Make SHADOW PUPPETS

NIGHT PATCH STICKERS

There are 12 patch stickers in the back of this book that match **I SEE IT!** circles on some of the pages. When you see an animal, a plant, or an object in the sky that matches something on an **I SEE IT!** page, put the sticker on the matching circle. See how many you can find!

Place the sticker on the circle!

Moths

I SEE IT!

A MOTH ENTERS THE WORLD AS A TINY EGG. A hungry caterpillar pops out of that egg and goes looking for leaves to munch. When it grows big enough, it makes a cocoon where it slowly changes into a winged adult. Most moths prefer to travel at night, unlike butterflies, which are active during the day. Another cool thing about moths? They taste with their feet!

White-lined Sphinx Moth

To sip nectar, a moth uncoils its thin proboscis and uses it like a straw.

Can you find any of these **MOTHS**?

Giant Leopard Moth

Cecropia Moth

Garden Tiger Moth

Moths rest with their wings spread out while butterflies rest with their wings tucked together.

Most moths are not as colorful as butterflies.

Polyphemus Moth

Have you ever seen moths fluttering around a light?

Tussock Moth

Luna Moth

Would you rather be a butterfly or a moth?

Closer Look

Moths have furry, comb-like antennae. Butterfly antennae are smooth with knobs at the ends.

13

NIGHTTIME DISCOVERY TIPS

LEARN to look for constellations in the sky.

USE YOUR EARS! Listen for chirping crickets, hooting owls, and singing frogs.

APPLY INSECT REPELLENT if it's buggy out.

IF YOU PICK UP A LIVING CREATURE, hold it for only a moment and then gently put it back where you found it.

MOVE SLOWLY and watch your step.

The Moon

THE MOON IS A BIG BALL OF ROCK that orbits around Earth. *Orbit* means "to move in a curved path around a planet or star." Even though it looks bright in the night sky, the moon does not produce its own light. What you see is the sun's light reflecting off the surface of the moon. The moon may look like a glowing ball or a narrow crescent, depending on what part of it is catching the sun's light.

Our moon is about a quarter the size of Earth.

A **super moon** looks bigger than normal because its orbit brings it closer to Earth.

DO YOU KNOW these special names for the moon?

A **blood moon** looks dark red during a total lunar eclipse. That's when Earth lines up between the moon and the sun and blocks the sunlight from hitting the moon for a short time.

A **harvest moon** is a bright full moon that occurs around the beginning of autumn.

The word **lunar** means "related to the moon."

A **moon halo** occurs when ice crystals in the atmosphere reflect light and create a giant ring or halo around the moon.

A **blue moon** isn't blue! It's just what we call a full moon when it's the second one to appear in a single month. This only happens every few years.

Closer Look

Look up at a full moon. Can you see the craters and mountains on its surface? Have you ever seen a face looking down at you?

THE PHASES OF THE MOON

You have probably noticed that the moon looks a little different each time you see it. One night it's a big round ball, another night it's a slender sliver. These different shapes are called the phases of the moon.

Sun

Moon

Earth

one revolution = 27 days

one revolution = one year

The moon orbits around Earth and reflects light from the sun. It takes the moon about a month to entirely circle Earth. Every day it's in a slightly different spot. And we can only see the part of the moon lit up by the sun. When the moon is full, we can see one whole side. When the moon is new, we can't see it at all because the part of it that faces Earth is not lit up by the sun.

Last Quarter

Waning Crescent

Waning Gibbous

Earth

New Moon

Full Moon

Waxing Crescent

Waxing Gibbous

First Quarter

LEARN THE TERMS!

The different phases of the moon have different names.

NEW—can't be seen at all

CRESCENT—less than half full and looks like a thin sliver

WAXING—getting bigger each night

GIBBOUS—more than half full

FULL—looks like a big perfect circle

WANING—getting smaller each night

Owls

OWLS ARE AMAZING HUNTERS. They have excellent hearing and night vision. They are not as fast as other birds of prey, but they are silent and stealthy. Their special soft feathers make no sound as they fly toward their prey and snatch it up with powerful talons. Some owls eat their dinner whole, then vomit up the fur and bones in little balls called pellets.

An owl can rotate its head to look behind its back!

Barred Owl

Have you seen or heard an OWL AT NIGHT?

Like all raptors, owls have sharp, curved beaks.

Elf Owl

Tiny elf owls nest inside big cacti.

Burrowing Owl

Barn Owl

Instead of hooting, barn owls hiss.

Great gray owls are almost three feet tall!

Great Gray Owl

Great Horned Owl

Closer Look

If you find an owl pellet under a tree, look for tiny rodent bones and teeth inside.

NOISES IN THE NIGHT

Try imitating the calls of these creatures that are active after dark. Hint: Ask an adult to pull up some animal calls online so you can practice.

WHO'S THAT?

Barred owls make a call that is easy to imitate. Try hooting in a deep voice, "Who cooks for you? Who cooks for youuuuuu?"

HOWL LIKE A WOLF

Put your head back and let out a long, slow howl. Did any neighborhood dogs or coyotes join in?

MOO LIKE A . . . FROG?

Bullfrogs make a deep croaking noise that sounds kind of like a mooing cow. Some people say it sounds like "jug o' rum, jug o' rum." What else could they be saying?

LISTEN UP

Your sense of hearing becomes extra-important in the dark when your eyes can't see well. Listen closely to what is happening around you. Check off each noise you hear.

Buzzing mosquito ☐

Rustling leaves ☐

Barking dog ☐

Wailing siren ☐

Running water ☐

Blowing wind ☐

Chirping crickets ☐

Hooting owl ☐

Swooshing car ☐

Moths

A MOTH ENTERS THE WORLD AS A TINY EGG. A hungry caterpillar pops out of that egg and goes looking for leaves to munch. When it grows big enough, it makes a cocoon where it slowly changes into a winged adult. Most moths prefer to travel at night, unlike butterflies, which are active during the day. Another cool thing about moths? They taste with their feet!

White-lined Sphinx Moth

To sip nectar, a moth uncoils its thin proboscis and uses it like a straw.

Can you find any of these **MOTHS**?

Giant Leopard Moth

Cecropia Moth

Garden Tiger Moth

Moths rest with their wings spread out while butterflies rest with their wings tucked together.

Most moths are not as colorful as butterflies.

Polyphemus Moth

Have you ever seen moths fluttering around a light?

Tussock Moth

Luna Moth

Would you rather be a butterfly or a moth?

Closer Look

Moths have furry, comb-like antennae. Butterfly antennae are smooth with knobs at the ends.

MOTH WATCH!

You can attract moths with light or a yummy smell! Set up a station to get a closer look at these amazing insects.

NOCTURNAL means "active at night."

LIGHT UP THE NIGHT

Moths will fly toward just about any bright light. Set up a lantern or flashlight outside, or stand under a porch light or streetlamp. The moths need a place to land, so bring along a white sheet (a white shirt or large piece of light-colored paper works, too) and hang or spread it out under the light. Now sit back and wait to see who shows up!

SWEET SMELLS

Moths also love the smell of ripe fruit. To give your winged friends a snack, mash up an overripe banana or peach in a jar and sprinkle 3 or 4 tablespoons of brown sugar on top. Mix in enough fruit juice to make a thick liquid.

Let the mixture sit in a warm place all day. In the late afternoon, spread the mixture with a paintbrush on a tree trunk or log.

Check your sugaring spot several times starting at dusk.

You can also try leaving out some plain mashed banana. Which bait attracts more moths?

The Stars

A STAR IS A HUGE BALL OF BURNING GAS IN SPACE. Our sun is the closest star to Earth. Most stars are about the same size as our sun, but because they are much farther away, they look tiny in comparison.

Stars appear white, but they come in different colors depending on how hot they burn. Blue and white stars are the hottest and they burn out the fastest. Red and orange stars burn at cooler temperatures, so they shine the longest.

The stars you see are trillions of miles away!

Have you seen any of these **CONSTELLATIONS**?

Look for Aquila in the summer sky.

For thousands of years, people have told stories about the constellations, which are groups of stars that form shapes.

Do you see Orion's belt?

Aquila (eagle)

Orion (hunter)

An astronomer studies stars and space.

The **Big Dipper** looks like a giant ladle. It's part of a larger constellation, Ursa Major.

Ursa Major (bear)

Pegasus (winged horse)

You can find Pegasus in the autumn sky.

Closer Look

The North Star, or Polaris, can be seen in the sky all year long. Can you find it?

Little Dipper

Big Dipper

North Star

LOOK UP & BE AMAZED!

The moon, stars, and planets aren't the only cool things you can see in the night sky.

NORTHERN LIGHTS

Imagine a moving painting of swirling colors across the dark night sky. This dazzling show occurs when the sun sends out a bunch of electrically charged particles called a solar wind. Sometimes when those particles come close to Earth's atmosphere, they create color and light.

COMETS

Comets are big chunks of ice and dust that orbit around the sun. They have two long tails made of gas and dust that stream behind them for millions of miles! A comet is only visible to us when it comes close to Earth. Some comets only get that close once in hundreds or even thousands of years.

MILKY WAY GALAXY

The Milky Way is a huge spiral of stars, dust, and gas. It's also our home in the universe. From Earth it looks like a giant fuzzy space cloud stretching across the sky. You need to be away from city lights to see this beautiful sight. The darker the better!

INTERNATIONAL SPACE STATION

Astronauts live on this station for months at a time while they work on scientific research and do experiments in space. From Earth, the station looks like a slow-moving bright white dot gliding across the sky. Even though they can't see you, it's still fun to wave at the people up there.

Amphibians

FROGS, TOADS, AND SALAMANDERS ARE AMPHIBIANS. That means they can live both on land and in water. Most hatch from underwater eggs and spend several weeks swimming around as tadpoles and breathing through gills before they grow legs and lungs and can survive on land.

Amphibians tend to rest during the day, hiding from predators and intense sunlight that can dry out their wet skin. They come out at night to hunt for insects, mate, and explore.

Frogs and toads croak and sing to attract mates.

What kinds of **AMPHIBIANS** have you seen?

Amphibians stay near water to keep their skin damp.

American Toad

Bullfrog

Singing spring peepers make ponds noisy places at night!

Tadpole

Red Eft

Spring Peeper

Spotted Salamander

Look out for salamanders crossing the road on warm spring nights.

Tiger Salamander

Closer Look

Most male frogs have a throat pouch, or vocal sac, that they inflate like a balloon to make their call louder.

Raccoons

RACCOONS ARE TRUE NOCTURNAL ANIMALS, so you're most likely to see one after dark. They live in many places, from forests and wetlands to big cities and backyards. And they will eat almost anything! Fruits, nuts, bugs, berries, bird eggs, crayfish, frogs, cat food, leftover pizza pulled from a trash can—just about anything!

Raccoons are very smart, have excellent memories, and are good at solving problems.

Have you seen any other **NOCTURNAL MAMMALS**?

Northern Flying Squirrel

Flying squirrels don't really fly, but they can glide between trees.

Armadillo means "little armored one" in Spanish.

Nine-banded Armadillo

Beware! Porcupines and skunks are masters of defense.

North American Porcupine

Striped skunk

Baby opossums ride on mama's back!

Opossums

Raccoons use their sensitive paws to handle and identify items that are good to eat.

Closer Look

GLOW-IN-THE-DARK EYES

Have you ever been riding in a car at night and seen a pair of eyes shining in the headlights? Or maybe you've taken a flash photo of your dog or cat and seen their spooky eyes glowing back at you? That's called eyeshine.

HOW ANIMALS SEE

Many animals have a lining at the back of their eyes that reflects light. It helps them see better in the dark. Those glowing eyes may look white, yellow, blue, green, or even red!

Human eyes don't have that special layer, so they don't appear to glow in the dark.

HOW WE SEE

Humans need light to see. When light enters your eye, it sends a signal to your brain. Then your brain tells you what you are looking at.

Look at your eye in a mirror or look at a friend's eye. See that little black dot in the middle? That is your pupil, which is an opening at the front of your eye. The colored part is called the iris. The iris can make the pupil bigger or smaller to allow more or less light in.

When it's dark, your pupils open wide to let in as much light as they can. In bright light, your pupils shrink so too much light doesn't hurt your eyes.

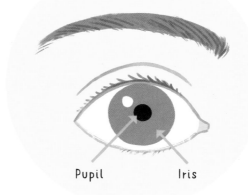

EYE IN LIGHT

Pupil   Iris

Notice the differences!

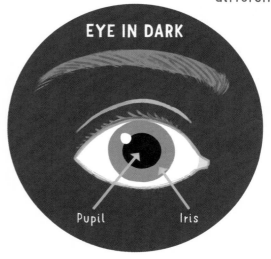

EYE IN DARK

Pupil   Iris

NOW YOU TRY

Grab a mirror or sit face-to-face with a friend. Sit in the dark for a few minutes, then quickly turn on the light or shine a flashlight in your face. Can you see your pupil go from big to small?

Crickets

ONE OF THE BEST SOUNDS YOU'LL HEAR ON A SUMMER NIGHT IS CRICKETS CHIRPING. Males make this music by rubbing one wing against the other. They make different chirps to attract females or scare off other males. How fast they sing depends on the weather. When the temperature gets cooler, their chirping slows down.

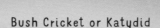

Bush Cricket or Katydid

Crickets have tiny ears on their front legs.

Look and listen for some of these other NIGHTTIME CREATURES.

Field Cricket

Fireflies can make their bellies glow!

Firefly

Periodic Cicada

Shy millipedes like damp places.

Millipede

Annual Cicada

A buzzing mosquito beats its wings 1,000 times a minute!

Mosquito

Tree Cricket

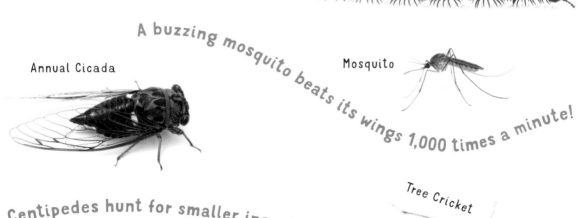

Centipedes hunt for smaller insects to eat.

House Centipede

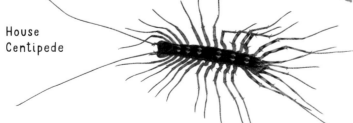

Closer Look

Can you see how a cricket's strong hind legs are bent and made for jumping?

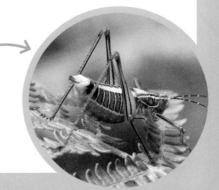

Glowworm

THINGS THAT GLOW IN THE DARK

Some creatures glow in the dark! This ability is called bioluminescence [by-oh-loo-mihn-EHS-ehns]. These organisms make their own light by creating a chemical reaction in their bodies. Some animals glow to communicate with others, attract prey, or escape predators.

IN THE AIR

Fireflies, or lightning bugs, are beetles, not flies. Scientists think they glow to attract mates. Have you seen fireflies zooming around on a warm summer night? Try catching one in your hands.

ON THE GROUND

Softly glowing jack-o'-lantern mushrooms grow in forests in North America, Europe, and parts of Africa. Different types of glowing fungus that grow in parts of South America and Asia look like nightlights in the jungle.

Look at but don't touch mushrooms. Some are poisonous!

IN THE OCEAN

The ocean is full of amazing glowing creatures like lanternfish, comb jellyfish, gulper eels, and certain types of coral, clams, and krill. You probably won't see them on your night adventure unless you are on a boat or a dock or walking on a beach at the right time. Or better yet, in a submarine!

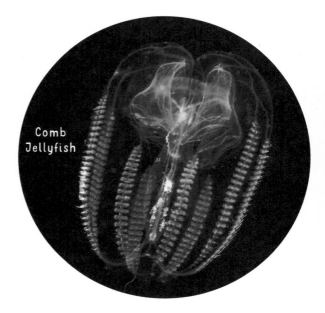

Comb Jellyfish

Bioluminescent tides occur when waves disturb tiny phytoplankton, causing them to glow.

The Planets

ALL PLANETS ARE ROUND, AND THEY ALL ORBIT AROUND THE SUN. In addition to Earth, there are seven main planets in our solar system. You can see five of them without a telescope: Jupiter, Venus, Saturn, Mars, and Mercury. Neptune and Uranus are too far away.

Because planets circle the sun at different rates, they are hidden from our view at certain times of year.

Stars seem to twinkle but planets do not.

Have you seen any of these **PLANETS** in the night sky?

Saturn

Uranus

Neptune and **Uranus** are too far from Earth to be seen by eye alone.

Neptune

Jupiter

Earth

Earth looks blue from outer space.

Mercury is hard to see because it is close to the sun.

SUN

Venus shines bright white in the sky.

Mercury

Venus

Mars

Moon

Mars

Can you find something glowing **orange** among the stars? That could be **Mars**!

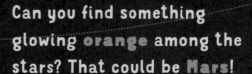

Closer Look

Jupiter is the biggest planet in our solar system.

SHADOW PUPPET FUN

Whether you're under a streetlamp, in a tent, or cozy in bed, playing with light and shadows is fun! All you need is a light source and your own hands.

bunny

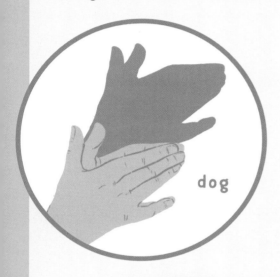

dog

Put one or both of your hands between the light and a flat surface so you can see a clear hand shadow. Try bending your fingers to make a bunny, bird, spider, or dog.

spider

bird

Have a grown-up shine a big flashlight on a wall or sheet so you can make puppet animals.

Grab a friend and make shadow shapes under a streetlight.

Make up your own shapes and

Bats

BATS ARE THE ONLY MAMMALS THAT CAN FLY.
They are found all over the world. Some bats
are smaller than a mouse and weigh less than a
penny, while others have five-foot wingspans!
Some eat fruit or flower nectar, but the bats
you're likely to see whizzing overhead are
probably looking for insects. They eat millions
of bugs every night.

Some bats
can eat 1,200
mosquitoes
in an hour!

Pallid Bat
drinking water

Have you seen **BATS SWOOPING** overhead?

Northern Long-eared Bat

A bat's heart beats 1,000 times a minute in flight.

Little Brown Bat

California Leaf-nosed Bat

Bats sleep hanging upside down.

Parti-colored Bat

Fruit Bat

Some bats are important pollinators for blooming plants.

Closer Look

A bat's wing is its hand! Their wings are made of a thin skin stretched between four long finger bones and a thumb.

NIGHT GAMES

If you're camping with family or hanging out with friends in your yard or at a park after dark, try some of these night games for group fun. Some are good for running around, others for sitting still.

GHOST IN THE GRAVEYARD

Start by picking a safe home base spot. A porch or tree will do. Pick one ghost who will go hide while everyone else counts to 100. When the group is done counting, they call "Midnight, moonlight, I hope to see a ghost tonight!" as they go looking for the ghost.

When a person finds the ghost, they yell "Ghost in the graveyard! Run!" All the players run toward the safe spot while the ghost chases them. The first person to get tagged by the ghost becomes the ghost next time.

A simple game of tag is extra fun if everyone has a small flashlight!

STORY TRAIN

Telling a story together is a great activity for when you're sitting around a campfire. One person starts by saying "Once upon a time . . ." The person next to them says a few more words, like "there was a coyote . . ." and the next person adds a few more words, like "who went looking for adventure . . ." Keep going around and around until you've told a funny or scary story together.

BEEHIVE

Pick two players, or bees, to hide in two different spots. These are their hives. Everyone else is a seeker. The seekers count to 100 and then go off in different directions looking for the hiders.

When a seeker bee finds a hiding bee, they quietly join them and huddle close in the hive. Each time a new seeker finds the hiders they also join the hive. Keep going until every bee finds a hive!

Deer

DEER EAT MOSTLY TWIGS, LEAVES, FRUIT, AND NUTS. They are crepuscular [creh-PUHS-kyoo-lahr] animals, which means they are most active at twilight. Look for deer by the side of the road if you're driving at night.

Baby deer are born covered in white spots. These markings help the fawns blend into their surroundings and keep hidden. The spots fade as they grow.

A male deer is called a buck, a female is a doe, and a baby is a fawn.

White-tailed Deer fawn

Have you seen any other large MAMMALS at night?

Red Fox

Coyote

Have you ever seen a deer leap over a fence?

Moose

Black bears are sometimes brown or even light tan.

Black Bear

Bobcats have short, thick tails.

Bobcat

Closer Look

Unlike horns, which never stop growing, a deer's antlers fall off in spring and grow back by autumn.

ANIMALS BY NIGHT AND DAY

The same habitat can seem quite different in the light or in the dark. See which animals sleep and which are out and about by day versus at night. How many can you count in each scene?

A **habitat** is a place where animals and plants live.

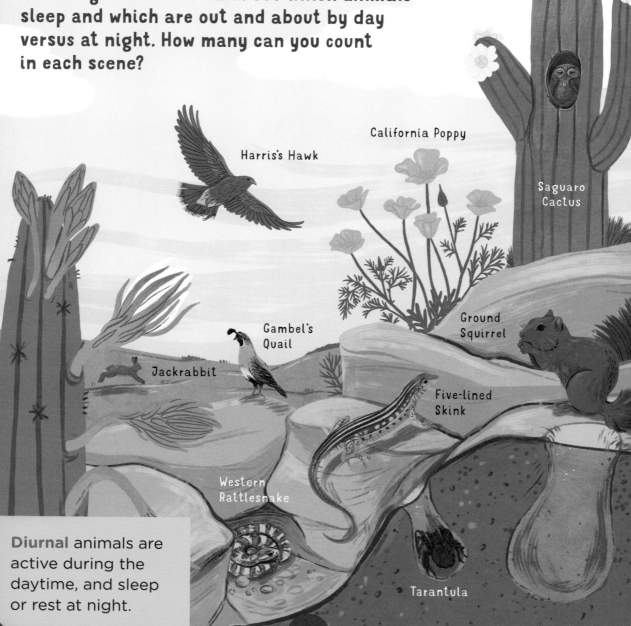

Harris's Hawk

California Poppy

Saguaro Cactus

Jackrabbit

Gambel's Quail

Ground Squirrel

Five-lined Skink

Western Rattlesnake

Tarantula

Diurnal animals are active during the daytime, and sleep or rest at night.

Nocturnal creatures travel and look for food at night and sleep during the day.

Elf Owl

Crepuscular animals are most active during the twilight of dawn and dusk.

Little Brown Bat

Night-blooming Cereus

Coyote

Kit Fox

Armadillo

Ringtail

Reptiles

LIZARDS, SNAKES, TURTLES, AND OTHER REPTILES are cold-blooded animals. This means they don't make their own body heat like mammals do. Instead, their body temperature depends on the temperature around them.

Most reptiles are active during the day so they can soak up the warmth of the sun, but some come out at night. Nocturnal reptiles emerge at dusk to look for food.

Baby Stinkpot Turtle

A turtle's shell is part of its skeleton!

Have you seen any of these **REPTILES**?

Reptiles hibernate in winter under soil, mud, or leaves.

Desert Rosy Boa

Scarlet Kingsnake

Many small lizards eat ants, grasshoppers, and other insects.

Gila Monster

Mediterranean House Gecko

Snapping Turtle

Eastern Mud Turtle

If you find a snapping turtle, look but don't touch. It might bite!

Closer Look

Reptiles have dry, scaly skin. See how different it looks from smooth, cool amphibian skin?

SHOOTING STARS

Have you ever seen a shooting star? You may already know it isn't an actual star, but what is it? There are a lot of big chunks of rock and metal floating around space. Sometimes a little piece breaks off and starts to fall toward Earth. We call that piece of rock or metal a **meteoroid**. The falling meteoroid moves so fast it burns up and heats the air around it. The long streak of light it creates is called a **meteor**.

Most meteoroids burn up in a few seconds, causing the meteor to disappear. If a meteoroid makes it all the way to Earth without burning up and hits the ground, it's called a **meteorite**.

During certain times of the year, you can look up on a clear night and see a bunch of meteors. This is called a **meteor shower**.

A meteor is a streak of light.

A meteor shower happens when many meteors fall at the same time.

A meteoroid is a chunk of falling rock or metal.

Most meteoroids are only the size of a small pebble or grain of rice!

A meteorite is what hits the ground.

LOOK AROUND

It can be tricky to find things at night! Use a flashlight or let your eyes adjust to the dark and see if you can find some of these things. Check off each one you find.

Moon ☐

Big Dipper ☐

Moths ☐

Eyeshine ☐

Streetlight ☐

Spiderweb ☐

Bats ☐

Airplane Lights ☐

Amphibians ☐

Night-Blooming Flowers

HAVE YOU EVER NOTICED that a dandelion opens its flower during the day, then closes tight at night? Most flowers do the same, but some plants only open their blossoms at night! Night bloomers are usually white or light-colored and have a strong, sweet scent that moths love. Some bats visit flowers at night looking for nectar, too.

Moonflower

Pale flowers reflect moonlight so night pollinators can find them more easily.

Have you seen or smelled any of these **BLOSSOMS**?

Try planting a moon garden with all white flowers.

Tuberose

Nicotiana

Evening Primrose

Saguaro

The Queen of the Night cactus blooms only once per year.

Night-blooming Jasmine

Can you find some closed-up blossoms?

Closer Look

Shine your flashlight into an open bloom. Can you see the dusty pollen?

CAMP OUT!

When you are outside, whether you are far from home, in your backyard, or out on a balcony, it's fun to go camping! Snuggle into a sleeping bag or make a nest of blankets on the ground. Wave a flashlight around or share stories with a friend. Listen for night noises or make up some of your own.

MY NIGHTTIME ACTIVITIES

Match up stickers to what you saw or did on your night walk.

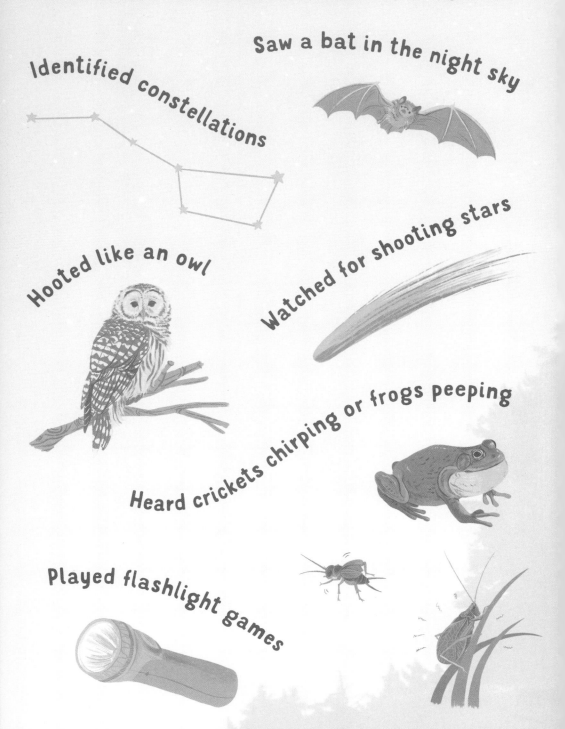

Saw a bat in the night sky

Identified constellations

Hooted like an owl

Watched for shooting stars

Heard crickets chirping or frogs peeping

Played flashlight games

MY NIGHTTIME ACTIVITIES

Match up stickers to what you saw or did on your night walk.

Made shadow puppets

Caught fireflies and let them go

Smelled a night-blooming flower

Told stories around a campfire

Found a salamander

Made a snack for moths

WHAT I LIKE ABOUT THE NIGHT

Write some words about being outside at night.
Was it fun? Scary? Exciting?

_____

_____

_____

_____

_____

Draw your favorite nocturnal animal.

MY NIGHT WALK LOG

Keep some notes about your nighttime adventures!

Date: _____ Time of night: _____

Weather: _____

What I saw or did: _____

_____

Date: _____ Time of night: _____

Weather: _____

What I saw or did: _____

_____

Date: _____ Time of night: _____

Weather: _____

What I saw or did: _____

_____

Date: _____ Time of night: _____

Weather: _____

What I saw or did: _____

_____

Date: _____ Time of night: _____

Weather: _____

What I saw or did: _____

_____

The mission of Storey Publishing is to serve our customers by publishing practical information that encourages personal independence in harmony with the environment.

Text by Katie Yale
Edited by Deanna F. Cook and Lisa H. Hiley
Art direction and book design by Erin Dawson

Text © 2024 by Storey Publishing

Storey books may be purchased in bulk for business, educational, or promotional use. Special editions or book excerpts can also be created to specification. For details, please contact your local bookseller or the Hachette Book Group Special Markets Department at special.markets@hbgusa.com.

Storey Publishing
210 MASS MoCA Way
North Adams, MA 01247
storey.com

Storey Publishing is an imprint of Workman Publishing, a division of Hachette Book Group, Inc., 1290 Avenue of the Americas, New York, NY 10104. The Storey Publishing name and logo are registered trademarks of Hachette Book Group, Inc.

Distributed in Europe by Hachette Livre, 58 rue Jean Bleuzen, 92 178 Vanves Cedex, France
Distributed in the United Kingdom by Hachette Book Group, UK, Carmelite House, 50 Victoria Embankment, London EC4Y 0DZ

ISBN: 978-1-63586-847-0 (paper over board with 3 sticker sheets, magnifying glass, and fold-out journal)

Printed in Dongguan, China by R. R. Donnelley on paper from responsible sources
10 9 8 7 6 5 4 3 2 1

APS

Library of Congress Cataloging-in-Publication Data on file